PIT BULLS ON GOLDEN STREET

Kevin R

PublishAmerica
Baltimore

© 2011 by Kevin Rottweiler.
All rights reserved. No part of this book may be reproduced, stored in a retrieval system or transmitted in any form or by any means without the prior written permission of the publishers, except by a reviewer who may quote brief passages in a review to be printed in a newspaper, magazine or journal.

First printing

PublishAmerica has allowed this work to remain exactly as the author intended, verbatim, without editorial input.

Hardcover 978-1-4626-0841-6
Softcover 978-1-4626-0840-9
PUBLISHED BY PUBLISHAMERICA, LLLP
www.publishamerica.com
Baltimore

Printed in the United States of America

Scripture taken from The New King James Version. Copyright© 1979, 1980, 1982 by Thomas Nelson, Inc. Used by permission. All rights reserved.

Dedication

This book is dedicated to Jo Jo the American Bulldog. Jo Jo was a victim of abuse and neglect. Jo Jo is now in Heaven, in the arms of the Creator.

PUPS

Loveable Pit Bull pups,
Heaven's drinking cup.
Leather skins;
Angels sing!

Born innocent,
Wrinkled days went;
Loving mother,
And the Heavenly Father.

These dogs sing,
Together in the barn.
Cuddly love they bring,
To God's farm.

MUSCULAR DOGS

Muscular dogs, enormous jaws,
Muscular dogs, mud on paws.

Muscular dogs with iron collars,
Muscular dogs, bark and holler.

Muscular dogs, eating from dishes,
Muscular dogs, with honest wishes.

Muscular dogs, strong and bold,
Muscular dogs, adopted and sold.

TOUGH DOGS

Tough-looking faces,
Scabs and scars.
Flared nostrils,
Roaming near cars.

Tan in color,
Bully-breeds.
Junkyard dogs,
Near railroad tracks.

Only seeking,
Chunks of meat.
Sky of gray,
Promoting steam.

Factories cry out,
Poverty and rain.
Bulldogs living,
In hungry pain.

Pit Bull paws, searching;
Rib cages inhale-exhale.
Moist eye buttons want love,
Butter cookies and garbage pails.

NUMB

They don't scare me,
I am numb.
Walking Pit Bulls,
Playing dumb.

Twenty Pit Bulls in-a-row,
Dumped here,
From dog pounds,
What a show!

Thick necks,
With dragon tails.
Fierce and ready,
Tough as nails.

Clouds, from their snouts,
Snowflakes on dry fur.
Paws imprinting…
Life's blur.

They don't scare me,
I am numb.
Walking Pit Bulls,
Playing dumb.

GROWLING

Labrador Mix,
Growling.
Avoiding eye-contact,
Miserable.

Lonely,
In metal cages.
Cement floors,
And dog toys.

Growling,
Foaming, nervous.
Circling,
Wolf ritual.

Labrador Mix,
Howling.
Avoiding dog biscuits,
Walking on egg-shells.

Icy stare,
Permanent glare;
Biting the metal fence,
Spraying urine everywhere.

RAINCOATS

Stormy seas and dog fleas;
Bulldogs wearing raincoats.

Thick necks and pectoralis major;
Bulldogs on boats.

No dry land in sight;
Bulldogs stay afloat.

Palm trees and coconuts;
Bulldogs sing music notes.

Salty seas only dampen hope;
Bulldogs want to go home.

Basset Hound made the trumpet sound;
Bulldogs depressed and alone.

Now the sky opened up;
Bulldogs with visions of twelve stones.

Jesus calmed the storm…
Bulldogs kneel at the throne.

HOT DOG CART

On New York streets,
Hot dog push carts struggle.

Nickel and dime economy,
Dogs without muzzles.

Salivate, push-and-shove,
Bulldogs sleeping in alleys.

Poverty and bully-breeds,
Hungry souls; trees without leaves.

Soaked in devil's moonlight,
Canines begging for meat.

The smell of Heavenly sausages,
Resurrect even the dinosaurs.

Dogs, born again, something to live for…
Rich man throwing hot dogs on the street.

Jaws like scissors,
Cutting up the spicy meat.

SATISFIED

Mastiffs…
Food bags
Muscular dogs
Salivate

Boxers…
Tin cans
Pink tongues
Smiling

German Shepherds…
Meat chunks
Tails wagging
Cheerful

Bulldogs…
Water dishes
Resting
Satisfied

ADDICTED

Pit Bulls,
Driving me insane;
Pit Bulls in the rain.

Pit Bulls,
In the car;
Pit Bulls on the farm.

Pit Bulls,
Wagging their tails;
Pit Bulls in dog jails.

Pit Bulls,
In my dreams;
Pit Bulls, peaches & cream.

Pit Bulls,
In the shower;
Pit Bulls smelling flowers.

Pit Bulls,
Walking everywhere;
Pit Bulls on the stairs.

Pit Bulls,
Kissing my chin;
Pit Bulls always win.

JO JO UPSTAIRS

Jo Jo went upstairs;
Climbed the dog ladder,
To Heaven.

Jo Jo meant well;
But life was shattered,
…a broken home.

Jo Jo tried so hard;
With tender eyes,
Kept his secrets.

Jo Jo jumped with joy;
For morning walks,
Blazing the trail.

Jo Jo was often gentle;
Sitting on his rump,
Waiting for dog biscuits.

Jo Jo the Bulldog;
Climbing the dog ladder,
To Heaven.

MORNING DOGS

Morning dogs,
After coffee,
Awaken my inner-child.

Morning dogs,
With sparkling eyes,
Powerful but mild.

Morning dogs,
Yawning, circling, embracing,
Mountains to climb.

Morning dogs,
Sunshine pokes through,
Fog on hazy trails.

Morning dogs,
Happy-go-lucky,
Pink tongues grin.

Morning dogs,
Back to their cages,
Together they sing.

BRUSHING MOLLY

Brushing Molly,
Quiet folly.

White pig skin,
Kissed-my-chin.

Pit Bull?
Dogo Argentino?

Very tame,
Never lame.
Senior dog,
A heavy log.

So cooperative,
Loves to live.

Always smiling,
Mostly quiet.

Everyone's friend,
Love to lend.

Offers a hug,
Eternal love bug.

SNOWED IN

Ice crystals,
Dogs, all snowed in,
A Malamute kissed my chin.

Ice crystals,
Frost on window panes,
Steam from a Great Dane.

Ice crystals,
Basset Hound singing,
Joyous trumpet, living.

Ice crystals,
Dogs, all snowed in,
A Shepherd like, Rin Tin Tin.

Ice crystals,
Paw prints escalate,
Ambitious dogs hesitate.

Ice crystals,
Dogs, all snowed in,
A Husky kissed my chin.

SHELTER DOGS

Neglected and rejected,
The smell of dogs;
Lonely depression, perfected.

Self-fulfilling prophecy,
"They need to be here,"
Abandonment and hypocrisy.

Some wag their tails,
Kissing pink tongues,
Unaware of this dog jail.

Pit Bulls, strong and bold,
Square cut jaws;
Lives, bought and sold.

Bully-breeds, musculature,
Honey Bun, Tiger and Theo…
Canine nomenclature.

Caged and hidden away,
Always risking,
Euthanasia, the very next day.

FORGOT HER NAME

It's been so long,
I forget her name,
An old song.

Sweet as honey,
Kissed my chin,
A Pit Bull puppy.

Climbing into my arms,
Pig skin jacket,
On the dog farm.

Sometimes she laughed,
Shyly looking away;
Enthusiastic dog bath.

A constant love bug,
Unconditional love,
Eternal belly rub.

ROOSTER

Parading like a rooster,
The tan dog with a black mask,
Penetrated my welcome wagon.
Growling, barking and jumping—
The new kid on the block.

Seeking food pellets or peanut butter,
Jaws like scissors never forget.
A spiritual cage with a rooster,
Longing for the softness of mother.

Nobody chooses to live here,
They get dumped as trash.
But making the best of it,
The rooster crows; life so brash.

Making friends with volunteers,
Or human jail guards,
Roosters cry canine tears.
A dog jail, with a prison yard.

They come to this sanctuary,
Under sunny skies.
Just hoping to leave by January,
Life filled with moans and cries.

PIT BULL RAIN

Rain, coming down, on moist backs,
Pit Bull rain.

Alone, near dumpsters, the rain attacks,
Pit Bull rain.

Junk yard dogs, without homes,
Pit Bull rain.

Dogs, that hunger for soup bones,
Pit Bull rain.

Dogs, pushed into fighting rings,
Pit Bull rain.

Dogs, praying for Heaven to sing,
Pit Bull rain.

Muscular animals, good creatures,
Pit Bull rain.

Muscular dogs, Heaven's features,
Pit Bull rain.

Dogs seeking God's love,
Pit Bull rain.

On death row, they push-and-shove,
Pit Bull rain.

JOYOUS MOTHER

The mother Pit Bull,
Wraps her newborn puppies,
With moist sunshine.

Kissing and licking,
Their innocent snouts,
Mother, loves her pups.

Defending them,
Guarding them,
Love to send.

Like leather jackets,
Tough puppies already,
Pig-skin tough.

The mother Pit Bull,
Teaching them,
To be good.

The mother Pit Bull,
Wraps her newborn puppies,
With moist sunshine.

PULLING ROPES

Now the fat Pit Bull,
Stood his ground.

Like a pig, a ham,
Sweating bullets.

Waiting for the rope,
Eternal rodeo.

Gripping the rope,
With sharp teeth.

A teething ring,
Oh, does his heart sing.

A gymnast,
An acrobat.

Like a soldier,
Never giving up.

Tug-o-war,
Pulling ropes.

KENNEL DAYS

Kennel days,
In a sunny haze.

Kennel flies,
Pasteur pies.

Water pails,
Hay bales.

Horses outside,
Cats hide.

Seeking shade,
And lemonade.

Big dogs for sale,
Empty water pails.

NEON LIGHTS

The old Boxer,
Like an old man,
Wrinkled.

Worried about,
A long bar tab;
Not enough to pay.

Neon lights,
Got the best of him;
Chasing lady dogs.

With a pool stick,
Yawning for morning;
Shuffling cards indoors.

Too old to play,
A game that never ends;
Neon lights.

Storefronts get lonely,
Dogs hang around;
Good night.

PIT BULL SOUP

The old horse had enough,
Taking bites from beaten creatures;
Riding high on sugar cubes.

The homeless Pit Bull,
Stalking the old horse;
Sometimes you have to change.

This day was different,
Nothing would stand in the way;
An old horse, just tired for sleep.

The Pit Bull, trying for the advantage…
As the old horse,
Invented Pit Bull soup.

And the music played,
"Amazing Grace,"
The old horse took his retirement.

SATURDAY

Choke collar
Muscular dogs
Dog baths

Muzzles
Clipping nails
Grooming salon

Children enthusiastic
Poodles
Hot dog dogs

SUNDAY

Church mice
Church rats

Outdoor dogs
Outdoor fleas

Indoor people
Bitterness
Seeking Jesus

MONDAY

The whole
Process
Starts over

Open cans
Feed the dogs
Poop bags

Never ending
But what a life
Loving dogs

STRONG LABRADOR

On the trail, Maize exploded;
"I don't like the leash," he declared.

So we fought a battle: tug-o-war;
But it wasn't a game, more that I could bare.

Back and forth with strong jaws;
Gripping the leash and energetic paws.

His eyes…were not of play;
They were on fire, a bad day.

I roped the leash to a tree;
Knotted it tightly for safety.

Used my cell phone to call;
The kennel manager, that's all.

They sent some help;
We got Maize back to his cage.

BLESSING OF PIT BULLS

Father in Heaven,
Please bless this Pit Bull dog.
Just as you blessed,
The other animals,
Under your care.
We know the strength,
Of St. Francis of Assisi.
He was a good shepherd,
Helping and saving the animals.

We also understand,
That Pit Bull dogs are very strong.
The breed can be dangerous,
In the wrong hands.

Father, we ask that you assist us,
That you put your hand on the dog,
And on the new Pit Bull owners.
Please guide them to a training program.

Father in Heaven,
Please bless this Pit Bull dog.
Just as you blessed,
The other animals,
Under your care.

Teach society about the goodness of dogs,
But also of the dangers and proper care of them.
We only want safety and protection from harm;
That people can have Pit Bulls if they want.

It is up to the public,
To receive proper training and obedience,
For bully-breed dogs.
Society must be responsible when living with dogs.

BRUTUS THE BOXER

What a day at the farm,
I almost lost my arm.

Brutus threw a fit,
And then he bit.

From the dog pound,
Never barked a sound.

Was quiet on the leash,
Short hair, like a peach.

The face of an old man,
Black muzzle and golden tan.

Was nervous and shaky,
A personality so flaky.

OUTDOOR PLAY YARD

Outdoors, it is sunny;
Dogs are funny.
Splashing in water,
Having fun.

Digging for bones,
Digging for gold,
Happy paws,
And strong jaws.

Pulling ropes,
Jumping rope;
Dancing and prancing,
Upward glancing.

Blinking eyes,
Barks and cries;
Rhyme and rhythm,
Happy season.

JUNK YARD

Ferocious-looking, muscular dogs;
Yawning, circling, paranoid.
Thick necks, as heavy as logs.

A Boxer carried a flying saucer;
His jaws and mouth exercising,
Only surround rusted scrap metal.

Now a German Shepherd stands guard;
His nose crinkling for scent.
Tough dogs, watching the junk yard.

The old Rottweiler sniffs his bowl;
Anticipating bloody meat,
Licking his fur…grooming ritual.

Onlookers take a peek often;
Observing the muscular animals.
These dogs…their hearts have hardened.

Don't expect any such slack;
They're out for blood,
And believe me, they will attack!

WINDOW OF DOGS

A rich lady,
Stands naked,
In the window.

Something isn't right,
And she is,
Right in the light.

The Mastiff surely,
Sees her,
Even he looks.

Elegant, showing off;
The dogs,
Always take a peek.

Her poodle,
Playing dumb.
Wishes to be unseen

Mastiffs yawn,
Thinking of old days;
Even dogs have pride.

HAMBURGER STAND

Bullmastiff chomping,
On hot hamburgers!
Fun, cheer—
A day of rollicking.

Just to lick,
Hot onions from his lips.
Onlookers impressed,
With olfactory glands.

Such a big dog,
Muscles ripping,
Under tan fur.
He also enjoys hot dogs!

Guarding and protecting,
But good with children.
Oh "Golden Arches,"
Embrace this dog with burgers!

Let him eat,
To his heart's content.
Jaws filled up with tender meat.
A life, so well spent.

BACK SEAT

The old Buick;
A dog car.
Always a Pit Bull,
Back there.

Moist snout,
Steaming up the windows.
Curious eyes,
But in a crate.
Excited, enthusiastic,
Wonder where…
We are going?
A dog park?

No, just to visit,
Grandma and grandpa.
Waiting patiently,
At the retirement community.

The old Buick,
A dog car.
Always a Pit Bull,
Back there.

AUTUMN LEAVES

Autumn leaves crunching;
The sky an eternal blue,
Bully-breed dogs, munching.

Digging holes in fresh soil;
Thick necks and iron collars.
Tired kennel workers, toil.

Glancing, prancing, singing;
Pit Bull dogs sniffing old shoes,
Hoping for love-bringing (home).

Chain-linked fence defines the law;
Stuck in a cat and dog shelter.
Wagging tails, but confused paws.

College students help the dogs;
Nobody wants to be a veterinarian—
Only to poop-scoop and play guitar.
Dog breath, snout air and clouds;
Prepare the soil for winter snow.
Caterpillars spin warm blankets.

JUST LARGE DOGS

Meaty, chunky, sweating;
Just large dogs.

Salivating, smiling, and pooping;
Just large dogs.

Black muzzles, glancing;
Just large dogs.

Powerfully built and muscular;
Just large dogs.

Oil glands, moist fur, snags,
Just large dogs.

Tough, rough-house types;
Just large dogs.

Guarding and protecting;
Just large dogs.

Just large dogs;
Just large dogs.

GOLDEN PAVEMENT

Fresh cement was poured,
But the Bullmastiff got out.
The large dog giggled.

Like Heaven's streets,
The avenue turned gold.
The Bullmastiff's tail wiggled.

Paw prints, paw prints;
Like the dog enjoyed it.
Leaving Bullmastiff imprints.

Maggie looked over her shoulder;
Catching a glimpse of Noah,
Reassured of no rain today.

So the dog gave her autograph;
Another paw print of identity,
Just a fun time, giggling.

But horseplay had its cost…tragedy.
She was run over by a truck,
And Maggie now boards the dog ramp.

Up to Heaven, she joyfully climbs.
Noah promised to care of her…
With paw prints on golden pavement.

SUNDAY MORNING

"Look at the dogs," the children declared;
Bully-breeds with honest eyes.
Now the Pit Bulls gained a stare.
At church, tails wagging everywhere!

Up the aisle, powerful dogs went;
Baring souls, confessing sins and worshipping.
Dogs asking for second chances, to repent;
The choir assisted a Basset Hound, with a trumpet sound.

Now the Mastiffs with big jaws;
Looked up to Heaven's gates,
Singing merrily and raising their paws.
An honest soul is never late.

RITA THE ROTTWEILER

Rita, a sweet gal;
Sat at the picnic table.
A working dog but domesticated,
Warm disposition and quite able.

Her life, mostly a party,
Retrieving biscuits and fresh meat.
Courageous, shy, and quite hardy.
A handsome gal, sitting at my feet.

Just wants to protect and defend;
Blinking eyes, yawning pink tongue.
Massages, belly rubs, with love to lend.
Warm sunshine and sitting on her rump.

Smiling takes up most of her time;
Shyly laughing, playing love games.
But paws are powerful, for digging.
Very muscular, a strong tower.

She peeks at birds and dragonflies;
Kind of understands nature.
Glancing with piercing eyes,
A wonderful gal, honest stature.

ROO

A tan Pit Bull baby;
I take to,
The senior center.

Sweet, shiny buttons;
Eyes of love,
Well behaved.

A warm bundle,
Love's answer,
Love-bug-cuddle.

So proud;
Roo visits the elderly,
Kissing with a pink tongue.

Projecting innocence;
With baby teeth,
Life is fresh, and so new.

Smelling flowers;
In the garden,
Roo pooped.

CROCODILE ARM

On the first week,
Volunteering at the shelter,
A Shar-Pei took me by surprise.

My muscles grew weak,
Fighting a dog in the street.
A crocodile on my arm.

He got me twelve times,
Up and down, up and down.
Surrealism gripping the leash.

Jaws like scissors,
Ripping the jacket to shreds,
Shaking his head like a shark.

On the first week,
I had a crocodile on my arm.
A bad day, at the dog farm.

BELLY RUB

Big dogs sitting on their rumps
Pull their feet forward
Belly down, roll over

Ecstasy, ecstasy, smiling dogs
Eyes peeking shyly
Pretending not to see

Only seeking another massage
Jaws open, smiling tongue
Head going side-to-side

The warmth of big dogs
Saliva dripping—
From talking snouts; no alphabet

Memorizing human faces
Remembering scents—
Big dogs sitting on their rumps

ANGELS

Hot breath in my face;
Big pink throats, smiling.
DOG spelled backwards is GOD,
I'm surrounded by angels.

Moist snouts, press against me;
Coming down from Heaven.
It's o.k. to wear blue jeans,
The kennel is my church.
A Bullmastiff showing affection;
Soft mouth and saliva glands,
I have tasted Heaven's gates.
Dog angels, an awesome ministry.

Mastiffs standing guard;
Protecting the Heavenly dog ladder,
Up above, is where dogs go.
I'm surrounded by angels.

Working with dogs can bring you fame,
Music, poetry, and the arts.
A dog kiss takes away the rain.
On rainbows, dog angels bark.

BULLDOG MOUNTAIN

When I pass away;
I'm going to Bulldog Mountain.
Blue skies and crystal fountains.

Jo Jo will be up there;
His paw in friendship, slap him five.
Up in Heaven, very much alive.

Children riding Bulldogs, on their backs;
An amusement park for everyone,
You will also meet God's Son.

So I'm headed to Bulldog Mountain;
With pig-skin dogs, humorous hams,
They never bite up there; they laugh.

Tails wagging, with faces of old men;
Tough old dogs went above,
Hurry; get your seat, push-and-shove.

When I pass away;
I'm going to Bulldog Mountain.
Blue skies and crystal fountains.

I LOVE THIS COUNTRY

The old Bulldog and I,
Cruising in my pick-up truck.
Going to find Jesus,
I love this country.

Raise the American flag,
In the back window.
With Jesus on my mind,
I love this country.

My Bulldog gave me a kiss,
Cruising in my pick-up truck.
Jesus is our friend,
I love this country.

My Bulldog wears a camouflage cap,
Sharing dreams and wishes.
Even tough-guys, can understand Jesus;
I love this country.

The old Bulldog and I,
Going fishing with Jesus.
Bread, charcoal and fish on the shore,
Man, I love this country.

KENNEL CAGES

Cement floors
Jumping dogs
Water pails
Bully-breeds

Boxers
Bullmastiffs
Pit Bulls
Bully-breeds

Yawning
Wagging
Smiling
Bully-breeds

Poop bags
Dirty rags
Grooming table
Bully-breeds

Bulldog
Rottweiler
Doberman
Bully-breeds

Sweating
Mopping
Scrubbing
Bully-breeds

BUCK THE PIT BULL

Licking ice cream cones,
Searching for dog bones.

Giving kisses,
And sniffing food dishes.

Tug-o-war ropes…
…Helps him cope.

Friendly as can be,
A "good boy" for you and me.

Pig-skin white,
Is visible at night.

Watched the world go by,
Would never hurt a fly.

Easy-going and happy-go-lucky,
A wonderful dog named Bucky.

Enjoys watching the sheep,
Always puts him to sleep.

TOUGH-GUYS

Tattoos
Chewing tobacco
Pumped on adrenalin
Bully-breed dogs
With Tough-guys

Pierced
On an alcohol buzz
Doing wrong things
Bully-breed dogs
With Tough-guys

Sinners
Criminals
Living in shadows
Bully-breed dogs
With Tough-guys

Liars
Cheats
Thieves
Bully-breed dogs
With Tough-guys

NOODLE

A very tiny woman;
Had trouble controlling,
Her Pit Bull dogs.

Confronting a neighbor man;
With Labrador strolling.
…Growling, snapping, and pulling.

The man struggled;
Attempting to separate,
Pit Bull dogs and Labrador.

Minutes turned eternal;
Punctured wrists and arms
An ambulance with sirens.

Pale and white;
The man's life,
Into the dark of night.

Whether Pit Bull or Poodle;
A very tiny woman,
Weak as a noodle.

LUCKY

I left you some biscuits
On your grave stone
I wish you were home

I got soaked in the rain
I saw your muddy footprints
I can't stand the pain

Your water bowl is empty
I see you standing there
And on the back stairs

Oh Lucky, you left me
Holding a broken leash
Always within reach
But I left you biscuits
They are your favorite
You know I always visit

GROOMING PIT BULLS

Theo smiled, and went into the tub;
Not concerned about soap suds.
So obedient and cooperative,
A life well lived.

Jo Jo the American Bulldog, also went.
Into the water, but never tense.
A beautiful gold and white,
His coat a wonderful sight.

Short-haired dogs escape the blow drying;
You won't see them crying.
They get a towel massage,
Excess water baggage.

Cleaning ears and clipping nails,
Chicken biscuits and wagging tails.
These dogs get a makeover—
Good looks and a beauty take over.

BOX CAR TRAIN

Huffing and puffing Pit Bulls,
Stacked to the ceiling.
So many; infinite.

Off to the killing rooms,
Society gives blame;
Rushing Pit Bulls to tombs.

Fearful eyes, the dogs cry.
Some guilty, some innocent;
Box car train, pounded by rain.

A tan baby dog whimpers,
Dozens of dogs on top;
Society wants the biting to stop.

Jo Jo peeks through the piles,
Of living meat; all warm dogs,
Blamed by society.

Only Heaven gives room,
For true justice;
Huffing and puffing, to their tombs.

EMERGENCY ROOM

A kennel worker;
To the emergency room,
A few stitches.
Breaking up dogs;
Mad at each other,
Irritated and restless.

Tiles, stethoscopes, sheets;
An X-Ray,
Sutures and medicine.

But they love dogs;
For good or worse,
Doing the best they can.

A kennel worker;
To the emergency room,
A few stitches.

CANDY STORE

Baby Pit Bulls,
With a sweet tooth.
Broke into the
Old-fashioned candy store.

Sucking Coca Cola from
Miniature soda bottles,
And wearing wax lips.

Tails vigorously propelled,
Counting candy dots
On long paper rolls.

Salt water taffy
Only satisfies young stomachs;
Gizzards too new to understand.

The cotton candy perfume
In the air, blends with popcorn.
Smiling, smiling, little dogs.

Caramels, chewed to the bone,
Rock candy licked pure;
Baby Pit Bulls, on their way home.

EYES

Dog eyes, peeking from cages;
Seeking help from people,
Looking and looking.

So many dog eyes, I have seen;
Tough dogs, bully-breeds and muscle-dogs.
Begging for love and attention.

Only to be heard, just a glance;
Candy for their souls,
Hearts warmed by human sunshine.

Now they just keep looking;
A Boxer smiles, a Rottweiler yawns,
Looking and looking.

Dog eyes, peeking from cages;
Seeking help from people,
Looking and looking.

BAD DOGS

A child is placed on a ventilator;
The staff physician was up all night,
You know how hospitals smell.

Another dog attack;
It took several men to subdue the animal,
The news is always bad.

Who is responsible for this?
Who is at fault?
They always ask...why?

Now the child is getting worse;
An infection is setting in.
At three in the morning, where is God?

The police take the report,
About bad dogs,
Coming from alleys and evil places.

Bad dogs, bad dogs, they say;
Nobody is held accountable,
Nobody is ever held accountable.

Something has to be done;
People and dogs need training,
Something has to be done.

TAN DOG

A tan Boxer;
With the face of an old man.
Weather-beaten and down-trodden.
Seeking shelter from the pain.

The tan Boxer;
A homeless animal, labeled by social norms.
Biting through cages, mad at dogs,
Seeking shelter from the pain.

A tan Boxer;
Got a bloody nose, banging his snout,
Against the cage of ferocious animals.
Seeking shelter from the pain.

The tan Boxer;
Gave me a kiss of anticipation,
For sunny skies and blue days.
Seeking shelter from the pain.

A tan Boxer;
Pushed around, abused and abandoned.
A living carcass and skinny.
Seeking shelter from the pain.

FIGHTING PIT

Ragged dogs; beaten and tortured,
Forced to support illegal fights.
Winding up in Satan's mortuary.

Stories of Bulldog and Terrier mixes;
A breeding ground of temptation.
Gaining popularity for hell's wishes.

Well-known in Europe and America,
Grown men, forking over betting money.
Climaxing in blood, guts and sabotage.

Early fighting pits; strewn with hate,
Gambling, booze, and tough-guys.
Puppies mature to an awful fate.

Dogs kept in a mildewed basement;
A gelatin-sweat on evil men,
Kicking the dogs…in a devil showroom.

And stories of bullbaiting;
Dogs attacking bulls, large animals.
For sports, for entertainment; selfish gain.

MUSCLES

The kids in the neighborhood
Avoided a dog named Muscles
Terrified of his powerful stature

Parading up and down
A chain-link fence
Watching every human activity
But one day, Joey got brave
Allowing Muscles to lick his ice-cream cone
Joey made extreme friends right away

Now Muscles enjoys candy corn
Kissing the children through the fence
A game of cat-and-mouse

Muscles escaped one rainy day
Dug a hole to get away
Sitting at the candy store; a sweet soul

THE DESERT

Vultures, pecking at salty meat;
Exposed rib cages and pig hooves.
Dog tails blowing in the wind.

Dead dogs tossed, into sandy graves;
From the fighting pits.
Bloody eye sockets, cry for mercy.

If Moses was here, he would pray;
And open the floodgates to Heaven,
Filling God's sunshine in an auburn sky.

Innocent dog bones, skeletons;
Cry out for tender mercy.
Now desert moles seek the cool water.

YELLOW JACKET

As the brindle-coat Mastiff
Retrieved the yellow tennis ball
He put his nose in the leaves
Unexpectedly poking the honeycomb

Now hundreds of yellow jackets
Like an army became airborne
Buzzing upward, buzzing upward
Released from the devil's pocket

Like hypodermic needles injected
The playful Mastiff was mesmerized
Became subjected to a trillion hormones
Now swollen, a war, nature rejected

The Mastiff scratched the moist soil
Afraid of an early grave
Out of breath; wheezing and boils
Frantic idiosyncrasy, a tough dog

Crawling to the back door
Grabbing the handle of metal
Just one glimpse to Heaven's sky
The Mastiff collapsed on the floor

FORGIVEN BY DOGS

Dogs I have sinned!
If we sin;
We still can win,
We are forgiven.

If we confess our sins,
He is faithful and just,
To forgive us our sins,
And to cleanse us,
From all unrighteousness.

(I John 1:9)

For I will be merciful,
To their unrighteousness,
And their sins,
And their lawless deeds,
I will remember no more.

(Hebrews 8:12)

Dogs I have sinned!
If we sin;
We still can win,
We are forgiven.

DIGGING HOLES

A bunch of
Bully-breed dogs
In the yard, bored

Digging holes
With muddy paws

A bunch of
Tough-looking dogs
In the yard, yawning

Digging holes
With muddy paws

Look, some holes
Are two-feet deep
Amazing, amazing

A bunch of
Bully-breed dogs
In the yard, bored

JO JO MY CHIROPRACTOR

With back trouble,
Jo Jo on-the-double—
Bent like a pretzel,
He jerked my back.

Pain into freedom,
Jo Jo my doctor—
Bent like a pretzel,
He helped my back.

On a Tuesday morning,
The first dog I see,
Sunny skies and lovely.
An American Bulldog.

Sometimes he would pull me,
Up the wooden staircase.
Built like an elephant,
An oxen, a whale!
A good old boy,
On the doggy trail.
Jo Jo my chiropractor,
Snapped my disk; a joy!

TROUBLE STREET

Starr, black Pit Bull Terrier
Leash-grabber
Growled and fought with me
Personality sweet and sour

Rita, Pit Bull Hound mix
Had to tie her to a mailbox
Growled, lunged
Was mean to me

Mercury, Shar-Pei with wrinkles
Got bit twelve times
Fought him on the leash
I was never afraid of him

Holly, a white Boxer
Chasing garbage trucks, aggressive
A one-man dog
Sweet with explosive character

Lucy the Rottweiler, with a cold stare
Like ice, cold, sneaky and paranoid
Never trust this one
Fixated on me, fixated, nervous

NUCLEAR DOGS

The agency had to recruit somebody
So Bully-breeds it was
Closing down a nuclear reactor
People on their knees

Pit Bulls glowing in the dark
Exposed to fluorescent doses
Summer came and went
Bald spots on their heads

Wearing masks and gowns
German Shepherds gave their all
Maneuvering the toxic waste
Wishing for puppy days

Oh, where is God dear city?
Mastiffs covered in bloody boils
Fighting a war of man-made strife
People on their knees

Dogs help the blind to see
Find people in avalanches
Assist the disabled
Fighting in wars and poverty

They have given their all
Pit Bulls glowing in the dark
Coming down from Heaven
In golden parachutes

Helping mankind
Doing the best they can
Fighting quicksand
Dog bones and a radioactive tan

FAST FOOD STREET

Rufus the Rottweiler
Grasping a chicken nugget
French fries in his jaws

Rex the Pit Bull
Engorging a Big Mac
But hungry for bacon

Buck the Pit Bull
Just pounding down
Pizza slice and pizza slice

Pooch the Mastiff
Kentucky Fried Chicken
He buried the bones

Jo Jo the American Bulldog
Sitting on his rump
You know how Bulldogs are

LEATHER DOG

At a musician's house,
A biker next door,
Keeps a leather dog.

Totally absorbed,
The dog engaged,
Digging up the yard.

The smell of engines,
Mufflers that vibrate,
They don't bother him.

Muddy paws sing,
As hamburgers cook,
Tattoos covered in oil.

Looks like a Rottweiler,
But a mask of black,
Could rip your heart out.

And the tough-lady,
She punches leather dog,
Takes him to the ground.

Showing who is boss,
Her whiskey voice attracts,
Other bikers around there.

At a musician's house,
A biker next door,
Keeps a leather dog.

COFFEE DOGS

I watch the dogs
From the window
Sipping coffee

Playing with one another
Tug-o-war ropes
Just chewing everything

The smell of coffee
Awakens my memory
Of old Bulldogs

Blue skies penetrate their retinas
Vascular brains want biscuits
Dog toys finally at rest

I watch the dogs
From the window
Sipping coffee

Submissive postures
Grooming rituals
Play bows and wagging tails

PIT BULL PRAYER

Please Lord, don't let
The hatred come alive
I don't want to fight

O God, the Lord
The strength of my salvation
You covered my head
In the day of battle

Do not grant, O Lord
The desires of the wicked
Deliver me, O Lord
From evil men

Those that plan evil things
In their hearts
They continually gather for war
Keep me, O Lord, from the wicked

Please Lord, don't let
The hatred come alive
I don't want to fight

(Psalm 140)

PAWS HELD UP

Pastor Bullmastiff prayed,
And the congregation sung.
Dog tails in rhythm, swayed.

Paws held up, to the sky;
Lift your paws in the sanctuary,
To bless the Lord.

Boxers, Pit Bulls and Mastiffs;
A Rottweiler bowed in prayer,
Music so wonderful and contagious.

Dogs, Bully-breeds in supplication,
Asking for second chances.
Jumping for joy, a Rottweiler dances.

Shedding their weather-beaten souls,
For a taste of Heaven's gates.
Lifting their paws in the sanctuary.

(Psalm 134:2)

SITTING ON HIS RUMP

Sitting on his rump,
Jo Jo waits for biscuits,
A finicky cat,
Just wants to sit.

No, he turned around,
Doesn't want to walk.
Never made a sound,
Sitting on his rump.

With a devotion,
To lunch meat,
Or hamburgers,
Sitting on his rump.

Salivating for meat;
And so patient,
He is satisfied,
With a special dog treat.

Sitting on his rump,
Sitting on his rump,
Just sitting on his rump.

ALONE

A German Shepherd,
Homeless and alone.
Searching for dog bones.

An old shoe brings scent;
Youthful reminder went,
Lost in faded memories.

They used you for wars,
Manipulated the police dogs.
Once a guard dog; life bent.

Water drips off your belly,
As the rain pours down,
With a hot spirit though.

Peeking through windows,
Grocery stores have meat.
3 AM, nobody on the street.

Old dog tags, like a veteran,
Hang from your neck;
Outdated and consecrated.

MY FRIEND JO JO

You were my sunshine
Of gold and white
You never tried to bite

You were my summer
You were my winter
A beautiful sight

You finally kissed my cheek
In front of the old Buick
Keeping your tenderness hidden

We had a relationship
You only tried to live
And society hurt you

But you were my friend
Just old fishing buddies
Once, you tried to be a tough-guy

But I saw your tenderness
And your puppy grin, from God
You accepted Heaven; now the angels sing

BULLBAITING

The bull scratches the earth
With mean hooves
And the Pit Bull prepares for war
The mud is soaked with rain

Pasture pies drain their smell
Muscular animals only want
A place called home
As evil men laugh in money

Allowing the gate to open
Pit Bull and cow emerge
A silver ring in a bull's nose
Both shiver in trembling spirit

Barn hay, dust, blood and mud
The bull fights like hell
Trying to keep the dog off his nose
The rawhide cow not pleasant

Enraged eye-sockets cry for mercy
The bull, the size of a tractor
Fighting off a Pit Bull dog
Gracefully defends his nature

Nobody wins in gambling games
Bloody water or barn yard fame
Cowboys, prostitutes and drunks
Only emerge from a smelly ranch

BAPTISMAL RAIN

Noah nervously counted the sheep,
As the devil's moonlight fell down.
Rain pelted the boat, mildew reeked.

But the smell of incense awakened me;
God's love only a heartbeat away—
Jesus and Pit Bulls upon the sea.

Oh, destroy all the wickedness;
The Lord gives second chances.
You were with us in the wilderness.

Bully-breed dogs covered in sin,
Bully-breed dogs never win,
Blamed by society; bites on shins.

As the rain pellets froze upon the deck,
The cows and chickens became dizzy.
Rain, baptism rain, second glances.

Pit Bull dogs, dancing aboard;
An ark of helplessness,
Begging God for special chances.

Heaven opens up, when there is death;
Jasper, sapphire and emerald stones cry out!
"God's glory will illuminate your soul."

Oh Lord, baptismal rain,
Make the Pit Bulls clean,
Your mercy in never-ending.

And the boat of our lives,
With its broken sails,
Is gracefully restored by Jesus Christ!

Oh, precious Lord, bring this ark,
To a place called Heaven,
And rescue us from the sharks.

BULLDOG THUMP

Bulldog thump,
Pit Bull dogs, on their rumps.
Bulldogs also on their rumps;
Thump, thump, thump.

Praise God with a trumpet,
Praise Him with lute and harp.
Praise God with dance,
Praise Him with stringed instruments.
Include some flutes,
But don't forget the loud cymbals.
Now everyone with breath praise the Lord!

Bulldog thump,
Pit Bull dogs, on their rumps.
Bulldogs also on their rumps;
Thump, thump, thump.

(Psalm 150)

DOG SUCCESS

In four years,
I have walked 4,000 dogs.
Bathed countless canines;
Was kissed by 1,000 dogs.

Had urine and poop,
In my eyes;
Surrounded by kennel flies.
Broken back and skinned my knees.

And through the tears,
Only suffered minor injuries;
Attacked by one, bit by five.
Numerous dog tongues on my lips.

The puppies give one hope;
In a world so downtrodden,
Giving purpose in a life well shod.
A dog kiss is Heaven's bliss.

BULLY-BREED MUSIC

Bullmastiff Maggie played a flute,
Propelling tails, nothing mute.
A white Bull Terrier getting down,
Nobody here wears a frown.

German Shepherd, danced with a lizard;
Bulldog spanking a mean old gizzard.
Everyone foaming at the mouth,
Its rock-and-roll canines from the south.

Break out now, with tails in the air;
A Pit Bull dog on harmonica.
Boxers and Mastiffs everywhere;
Rufus the Rottweiler, played melodica.

Singing, prancing and glancing,
A Bully-breed shuffle with dancing.
Life's only chance to "canine party,"
Your existence, like a Saturday night.

Christmas lights on the old dog house,
Basset Hound made the trumpet sound.
Jo Jo jammed on a plastic flute,
Bongo drums and a Malamute.

PRAISE HIM

Praise the Lord,
The maker of dogs.

Praise the Lord from the earth,
You great sea creatures,
And all the depths.
Fire and hail, snow and clouds;
Stormy wind, fulfilling His word;
Mountains and all hills;
Fruitful trees and all cedars.
Beasts and all cattle;
Creeping things and flying foul.

Praise the Lord,
The maker of dogs.

(Psalm 148: 7-10)

SOCIAL RESPONSIBILITY

If you must have a tough dog
Then please be responsible
Use collars, leashes and fences

Safety comes first
For you and the dog

They always blame a big dog
Or one with square-cut jaws

Safety comes first
For you and the dog

They always blame a Pit Bull
Or the Bully-breeds

If you must have a tough dog
Then please be responsible
Use collars, leashes and fences

Safety comes first
For you and the dog

Give him training
And obedience school
Don't be a fool

HUMOROUS HAMS

Look at the Bulldogs,
Such humorous hams.

Pugs are like that too.

Look at the Bulldogs,
Such humorous hams.

Sneaking cookies,
And drinking beer.

Look at the Bulldogs,
Such humorous hams.
Using all the toilet paper,
Making toy airplanes.

Wearing baseball caps,
And reading the newspaper.

Look at the Bulldogs,
Such humorous hams.

SWEETIE

What a tender dog,
I visit at the shelter.
Heavy as a log,
Her love unstoppable.

Digging a hole,
In the cool earth;
Comforting a new birth.

A hot "dog-kiss" again;
Her black mask-snout,
Like God spray painted her.

Just playing in sunshine;
Wanting to be friends,
And such love to lend.

Waiting for a new family;
She is so patient, so patient!
Pit Bull she is, but life stable.

What a tender dog,
I visit at the shelter.
Heavy as a log,
Her love unstoppable.

BURDICK STREET

I'm not a tough-guy,
But I feel strong,
On Burdick Street.

Thousands of dogs,
I have walked there,
On Burdick Street.

German Shepherds snapping,
Pit Bulls napping,
Bulldogs laughing.

Falls on the ice,
Injured by dogs,
On Burdick Street.

Their love is unconditional,
Kissed by a multitude of dogs,
On Burdick Street.

Bully-breeds on a leash,
Make me strong,
On Burdick Street.

COUNTRY DOGS

Sunshine on dog tails,
Labradors on dog trails.

Puppies grin for love,
Pit Bull babies, push-and-shove.

Kissing lemonade drips,
Honey on their lips.

A July day lasts forever,
Protected and groomed by mother.

Big and little dogs,
Begging for hot dogs.

And they salute an American flag,
Country dogs; their tails wag.

CITY DOGS

Sewer caps eject steam.
Overcrowding; Boxer with a mean face,
Garbage cans and muddy streams.

A plastic Barbie doll floating;
Too much hustle, too much bustle.
Cigar dangle; Mastiff smoking.
Neon lights bring evil people;
Dogs need to have an attitude,
Down here, no church steeples.

Stadiums, office towers and garter straps;
Dogs suffocate on outdated perfume.
People like mannequins, just pretend-smile.

Sirens, loud noises, slamming doors;
Bullmastiffs, just want grass to chew.
Humans; tainted sweat, from their pores.

Hard being a city animal;
Not scenic, too much cement.
Even the squirrels here, are cannibals.

POOCH MASTIFF

The big dog at the shelter;
We made friends right away!
Brindle coat; big head, large jaw.
He was gentle, gentle, with me.

Carried a basketball in his jaws;
Buried a dog bone, one sunny day.
Clear head and eye, "good boy,"
Just hoping for adoption today.

We always did the same walk;
He got a view of his surroundings.
To him I would talk,
Obedient, he sat, and rolled over.

Then, he asked me to be his master;
I felt so humble and proud.
He began guarding behavior,
Sitting right at my feet.

MAX

Just have to say something about Max
What a large black Labrador
We became a unit
Together as one

So loyal
Such friendship
He ate fresh grass
From my hands
Like a lover

Just have to say something about Max
What a large black Labrador
We became a unit
Together as one

So loyal
Such friendship
He ate fresh grass
From my hands
Like a lover

Just have to say something about Max
What a large black Labrador
We became a unit
Together as one

So loyal
Such friendship
He ate fresh grass
From my hands
Like a lover

Would you like to see your manuscript become a book?

If you are interested in becoming a PublishAmerica author, please submit your manuscript for possible publication to us at:

acquisitions@publishamerica.com

You may also mail in your manuscript to:

**PublishAmerica
PO Box 151
Frederick, MD 21705**

www.publishamerica.com

Lightning Source UK Ltd.
Milton Keynes UK
UKOW051019110712

195808UK00001B/49/P